JETLINERS
U*S*A

JETLINERS
U★S★A

Mark R Wagner and Christy Campbell

OSPREY
AEROSPACE

Acknowledgements

The authors would like to thank Bruce and Pauline Drum, Donald B Boyd, Bill Stubbs, Lonny P Craven, and Dan Fergen at Miami International Airport; John R Braden and Kimberly Foster at Atlanta International Airport; and David Wegman at Orlando International Airport. Finally, thanks to Scants, Frog, Pat, Rich and Smell for helping out during the various forays across America.

Published in 1992 by
Osprey Publishing Limited
Michelin House, Fulham Road, London SW3 6RB

Reprinted 1994

© Osprey Publishing

ISBN 1 85532 217 X

Editor Tony Holmes
Page design by Paul Kime
Printed in Hong Kong

This volume is dedicated to Fiona

Front cover This American Airlines MD-80 is about to hit the hot tarmac at Phoenix Sky Harbor Airport in Arizona

Back cover Delta has dominated the superhub of Atlanta, Georgia, since the demise of Eastern Airlines. Long lines of jets wearing the distinctive Delta house colours are not just a daily occurence but a constant feature of the airport today

Title page Boeing 757-225 of America West on approach to Phoenix Arizona's Sky Harbor airport. The registration N907AW can be made out on the nosewheel doors in this shot taken in February 1989. This aircraft was originally ordered by Eastern, but was diverted to America West in December 1987. A comparative newcomer to the US airline industry, America West only began operations in 1981 as a bright new hope of the newly de-regulated industry. A decade later it had become the tenth largest airline in the USA, with its annual revenues topping $1 billion. However, like several of its much older established rivals, America West too ran into deep financial trouble at the outset of 1991

For a catalogue of all books published by Osprey Aerospace please write to:

The Marketing Department, Octopus Illustrated Books, 1st Floor, Michelin House, 81 Fulham Road, London SW3 6RB

Above Tail feathers soon to be plucked – Eastern Boeing 757 tails line up at Miami International Airport in March 1990. The aircraft have had the maker's '757' logo removed from the fin as originally finished, and the stripe in company colours extended. Once, mighty Eastern (which had been launch customer for the 757 in January 1983) succumbed to financial disaster at the outset of 1991, its Miami-based South American and Caribbean services were sold to American Airlines. Miami, now a booming super-hub, was opened as 'Pan American Field' in 1928 on a site in what is now the north-east corner of the sprawling international airport. It swallowed up another field called '20th Street Airport', which is now the site of the main terminal building, and its present name was adopted in 1946

Introduction

This book captures in a series of stunning photographs the world's most dynamic industry – air transport – in its biggest market and most vibrant setting – the United States. But already it is a work of history whether it records the round-the-clock activities of a booming super-hub airport, or a sleepy day at some municipal commuter field. Many of the airlines and their aircraft caught on film in this book at the high tide of bold 'eighties expansion, have now gone into bankruptcy, having been gobbled up by their rivals or have become shrunken shadows of what they once were.

In 1991 hugely famous names like Pan Am and TWA virtually disappeared from the Atlantic, selling their landing rights at European destinations to the new big three, American, United and Delta. These airlines leapt from being major forces inside the USA to global mega-carriers. Northwest Air has made a late run to fourth position. These new giants have also moved to reinforce their position in Asia, opening dedicated hubs in Japan and preparing for a marketing battle with regional carriers chasing the boom in 'Pacific Rim' air travel.

And in America itself, names from the earliest days of US commercial air transport were driven to the wall. Companies like Eastern and Continental were stalked by Wall Street asset strippers, having to slash seat prices to compete while trimming routes, thus starving themselves of cash with which to buy new aircraft. At the same time, many of the new players on the domestic scene that bravely set up for business in the post-deregulation era that began in the early eighties – airlines like America West and Midway – were driven into bankruptcy or takeover by ruthless competition in the huge but perilous US internal market.

Two issues above all shaped the battle: the hub and spoke system by which many short-haul and commuter flights are fed into a hub airport and passengers transfer to a long distance flight; and the rise of the computer reservation system by which passengers are keyed automatically through a series of flights. In the battle of the check-in desk, American and United moved early to ensure that their systems, weighted not unnaturally towards their own services, were up and running first.

There were strikes and there were corporate raiders to contend with. There were fuel price hikes and new aircraft got to be very expensive, but it was the battle of the check-in desk which decided who would survive and who would perish. As well as joint marketing arrangements, the majors have also taken over or bought majority shareholdings in many of the US regional and commuter carriers feeding the spoke-lines to the hubs.

Hauling freight may not seem so glamorous, but what happened to passengers in the US airline battles also happened to parcels. There was a boom in the overnight package-freight business which pushed airlines like Federal Express and UPS to prominence, swallowing up independents like Flying Tigers. This book gives more than a glance at the US airfreight scene, from UPS DC-8s queueing at Atlanta to FedEx's bustling night-time Los Angeles package-central.

Throughout this period of seismic commericial upheaval in the airlines, the US aircraft industry has delivered some of its finest products, setting new standards in operating efficiency, safety and passenger comfort; jetliners like Boeing's 757 and 767, and McDonnell Douglas's MD-80 series. But for all their super fuel-efficient engines and two-man digital cockpits, the new generation of aircraft could not rescue even those airlines, like Eastern, who staked their futures on getting them into service first. The airline business moves fast, and nowhere faster than in America. This book captures the excitement of what some already see as its golden age.

Contents

Airlines meet at Burbank/Glendale/Pasadena airport in January 1989. A United Boeing 737-300 taxies to take-off while a Delta 737-300 awaits pushing back and an Alaska Airlines McDonnell Douglas MD-83, registered N930AS, is parked. Alaska Airlines, with its headquarters in Seattle, Washington state, has built itself into a major carrier along the US West Coast in just a few years. Originally founded as McGee Airways in 1932, the present name was adopted in 1944 as several smaller carriers in Alaska were swallowed up. The airline merged with Jet America in 1987, giving it a dominant position in the western states of California, Arizona, Idaho, Oregon, Washington and Alaska, where its largely Boeing 727 and MD-80 based fleet flies a demanding route schedule. Interchange agreements with American provide through-services from Anchorage and Fairbanks to Chicago, Dallas/Fort Worth and Washington DC

Boeing twins and trijets

Left Piedmont Airlines Boeing 727-214, N855N, climbs away from Runway 27 Left at Miami International Airport in March 1988. North Carolina-based Piedmont airlines was taken over by USAir in 1987 and its once highly individual marketing identity was submerged in 1989. This aircraft had been delivered to Pacific Southwest Airlines as N537PS in 1969, bought by Piedmont in 1981 and re-registered N855N in February 1988 and named *Dixie Pacemaker*. In USAir colours the aircraft was re-registered again as N719US

Below A busy morning in April 1990 at Atlanta's William B Hartsfield airport. Head of the take-off queue is an Eastern 727, followed by an Eastern Metro Express BAe Jetstream 31 and two United Parcel Service DC-8 Series 70 freighters looming behind. United Parcel Service (UPS) began major air operations in 1953 promising a two-day delivery time between major US cities. In 1982 the service went overnight and the company began to build up its large fleet of over 200 DC-8-71Fs and DC-8-73Fs, reworked and re-engined in the early 1980s as package freighters. The network was extended to Europe in 1985 and destinations in Asia, Japan and Australia were added in 1989

In balmier days before terminal
commercial troubles overtook
Eastern, a Boeing 727-200 rotates off
Runway 27 Right at Miami
International in March, 1988

Left Mid-town Manhattan looms behind bustling La Guardia, New York's domestic airport packed with airliners in an April 1991 shot taken from the Triboro' Bridge. Runway 31/13 runs parallel with the shorelines of Flushing Bay at this close-to-the-city airport (six miles from 42nd Street) built on a reclaimed rubbish dump in the Borough of Queens and hemmed in by the East River. The rusting of cans on the tip site caused big subsidence problems in the 1950s. New York's International airport, built on tidal meadows beside Jamaica Bay, was opened as Idlewild in 1949, but was renamed John F Kennedy in memory of the assassinated President in December 1963

Above Boldly finished in Pan Am's striking livery, Boeing 727-2B7 N202US *Clipper Blue Jacket* approaches the cross-runway at Miami International. This aircraft was already eighteen years old when caught by the camera in March 1988, and had passed through Allegheny, Braniff and Northwest Orient ownership, variously registered as N750VJ and N404BN. The very successful Boeing 727 tri-jet, the prototype of which first flew in 1963, had a production life of twenty-two years, and for a time was the world's highest selling jet transport with 1832 built, until overtaken as a sales success story by the same company's twin-jet 737. When launched in the early 1960s, the Boeing 727 ideally suited jet operations on short to medium range routes in the fast growing US domestic market. Its comparative quietness to other larger 1960s generation jets also allowed it to overcome the jet-ban at New York's La Guardia airport. United was the launch customer and several early buyers placed fleet renewal orders for late models sixteen years after the first deliveries. The last aircraft, a 727-252F package freighter for Federal Express, was completed in September 1984. Federal Express has subsequently modified its 727-252F purpose-built freighters with new engine hush-kits, allowing night operations into selected noise-regulated airports

Left The lush green hills dotted with tin-roofed houses behind Harry S Truman airport, Charlotte Amalie, on St Thomas, US Virgin Islands, frame this Boeing 727-200 of American Airlines. The aircraft, registered N703AA, first flew in May 1981. Here the camera catches it in March 1988 readying for take-off on the parallel taxiway to Runway 27 at this busy Caribbean vacation destination; a favourite for fly-cruise liner package operators

Above The scene at Miami International looking north from the terminal, captured in March 1988. In the foreground are Eastern 727, N8877Z, a 727 of Continental, registered N79749, Braniff 737 N4505W and an Eastern 727, registered N88742. All of these airlines were soon to be hit by commercial turmoil. In the distance, on the far side of Runway 27 Right, is a stripped down Boeing 707 with its nosecone missing, another 707 of Tampa Columbia, several Lockheed Electras, a 727, a 737-200, five IAI Aravas, four Cessna 402s and two DC-8s, and that is only a quarter of the ramp space that runs the length of Miami's NW36th Street

Above A Boeing 727 (N803SC) in the striking black scheme of the now defunct airline Suncoast, caught at Fort Lauderdale, Florida, in February 1988. This aircraft had passed through Braniff, Alaska and McClain Airlines' hands before its brief service with Suncoast from May 1987 to March the following year. It has since been operated by Avensa of Venezuela and the Costa Rican airline LACSA. In the background is the ill-fated Super Constellation which resided for many years on the 'Hill Ramp' during the late 1980s. An attempt to fly it out was aborted after two engines failed

Right Northwest Airlines Boeing 727-200 waits at Los Angeles, Terminal 2. Northwest is a major US carrier, with its traffic hubs at Detroit, Minneapolis/St Paul and Memphis flying a large domestic network within the USA and in Canada. The airline was founded in 1926 as an airmail carrier operating between Detroit and Minneapolis/St Paul. Slowly the airline, by now called 'Northwest Orient', began to build a spreading route network using a wide collection of aircraft. Postwar the airline built up a transcontinental route network within the USA flying from New York and Washington to Portland and Seattle, and out across the Pacific to Alaska, Hawaii, Japan and Korea. Boeing Stratocruisers were acquired in 1948, then DC-7Cs and Super Constellations followed in the mid-1950's. The first turboprops were Lockheed Electras and the first pure-jets, Douglas DC-8-30s, went into operation in 1960 followed two years later by Boeing 720Bs. Wide body 747-100s joined the Northwest Orient fleet in 1972 followed by DC-10-10s. Following de-regulation of the US airline industry in the late 1970s, Northwest moved to build up its route network, aggressively opening a service from Chicago to Tokyo and all-cargo flights across the north Atlantic. The airline was the launch customer for the Boeing 747-400 in 1989 when the first of these new generation, fuel efficient, 630-seaters went into service on the transpacific routes. Northwest also has large numbers of Airbus aircraft on order

Above Still wearing a hybrid colour scheme following the buy-out of Republic Airlines by Northwest in October 1986, Boeing 727-200 N2717 approaches Miami International's Runway 30 in March 1988. In 1985 the operator was commercially restructured and retitled plain Northwest Airlines, and began a dynamic period of expansion. It has marketing agreements with four commuter airlines, Big Sky, Express, Mesaba and Precision, which feed passengers to the hubs under the banner 'Northwest Airlink'

Left Boeing 727-200 N54331 of TWA rotates off Runway 25 at Las Vegas McCarran International Airport, February 1989

Above Late afternoon spring sunlight hits Miami International as a Braniff Boeing 727 climbs away from Runway 27 Right in March 1988. Braniff was an early casualty of the great post-deregulation US airline industry shake-out. In and out of financial crisis through the 1980s, the old-established Texas-based carrier filed for bankruptcy protection for the second time in 1989. The once-famous name was bought in 1990 by a group of businessmen and in July 1991 the airline was merged with Texas-based Emerald. Scheduled services were begun between New York, Orlando and Fort Lauderdale, Florida. But the rebirth was short lived as five weeks later Braniff filed for bankruptcy protection yet again

Left Caught by the camera in February 1989 on short finals to Runway 8 at Sky Harbor International Airport, this Boeing 727-200 of Alaska Airlines had been originally delivered to Braniff in February 1977, then operated by Alaska since April 1985. Sky Harbor was opened under that name in 1935 and became an international destination in 1970

A rainy night in Texas. A busy scene at Houston Intercontinental Airport in January 1989 as a Continental Boeing 737, then newly acquired from Frontier Airlines, is pushed back on the stand. In the background a Continental DC-10 completes its landing roll on Runway 8. Houston-based Continental Airlines, which at the end of the 1980s was the fourth largest US carrier, went into so-called 'Chapter 11' bankruptcy protection at the end of 1990 in an effort to buy time to restructure its finances, blaming its plight on the effect of the Gulf crisis and increasing fuel costs. Seven years earlier it had gone through a similar crisis but had survived. The airline traces its origin to July 1934 when it began operations as Varney Speed Lines. In 1937 Varney bought the Denver Pueblo route of Wyoming Air Service, moved to Denver and changed its name to Continental. The merger with Pioneer Airlines in 1955 and the granting of the Chicago-Los Angeles route via Denver marked its transition from a regional airline to a mainline operation, the first jets – Boeing 707-124s – appearing in 1960. In 1981 Texas Air bought a controlling interest and merged the airline with its own Texas International. In September 1983 Continental first filed for Chapter II protection, slashing its domestic route network from 78 points to 25, and its workforce by two-thirds. The airline clambered back into profit and in 1987 the operations of the People Express Group (Frontier, People Express, Britt Airways and Provincetown Boston Airlines) and New York Air were merged into Continental, doubling its size. In 1990 Continental operated to 82 US domestic and 42 international destinations from its four major hubs at Denver, Houston, Newark and Cleveland, fed by a web of feeder services under the name Continental Express. As its cash crisis deepened in 1990 Continental sold its Seattle-Tokyo route authority to American Airlines, but talks with Delta on other Pacific routes were not concluded. In late 1991 the airline was forced to make further cutbacks, trimming its Continental Express domestic-feeder operation

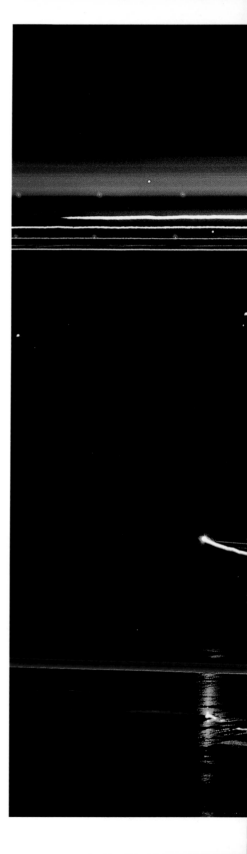

Left The glow of a Florida evening silhouettes a Boeing 727-200 on approach to Runway 9 Left, Miami International, in March 1988

Above On the ramp at John Wayne, Orange County California is a Boeing 737-300 of Continental Airlines, N17306. This aircraft had first been delivered to Texas Air Corporation in August 1985. The first of the highly successful Boeing 737 line, the model -100 flew for the first time in April 1967, but was quickly followed by the slightly stretched 737-200 in August the same year. Several noise reduction modifications for early Boeing 737s are available to enable them to meet new airport noise limit rules. From its first flight in February 1984, the 131-seat model -300 has become the best-selling version of the 737, and the reliability of its CFM56-3 engines has proven outstanding. The -300 also makes use of technology developed for the 757 and 767 programmes. The slightly stretched 150-seat 737-400 made its maiden flight in February 1988, with Piedmont (USAir) as launch customer

Overleaf Continental Boeing 737-300 at Miami International in March 1988. In the background is an Airbus A300. Continental has 17 European-built airliners in the fleet

Above Boeing 737-300 N334SW of Southwest Airlines, dubbed 'Shamu', in striking 'Seaworld of Texas killer whale' paint scheme at Love Field Dallas, in summer 1988. Dallas-based Southwest was founded in 1967 as a Texas regional airline and today it has expanded to operate its large fleet of 737-200s and -300s to 31 US airports in 14 states

Left N333SW Boeing 737-300 of Southwest Airlines departs Las Vegas McCarran International Airport's 12,636-foot long Runway 25 in March 1989. Hot and high operating conditions (McCarran, on its present site since 1948, is 2000 feet above sea level in the Nevada desert) spells the need for this airport's long runways

Above The glow of a southern Californian evening in January 1989 bathes N322UA, Boeing 737-322 of United Airlines at John Wayne Airport, Grange County. This aircraft was delivered in May 1988

Right Foreshortened by the camera angle, this United Airlines Boeing 737-300 is caught on short finals to the 12,000-foot long Runway 11 Left, at Tuscon International, Arizona, in February 1989

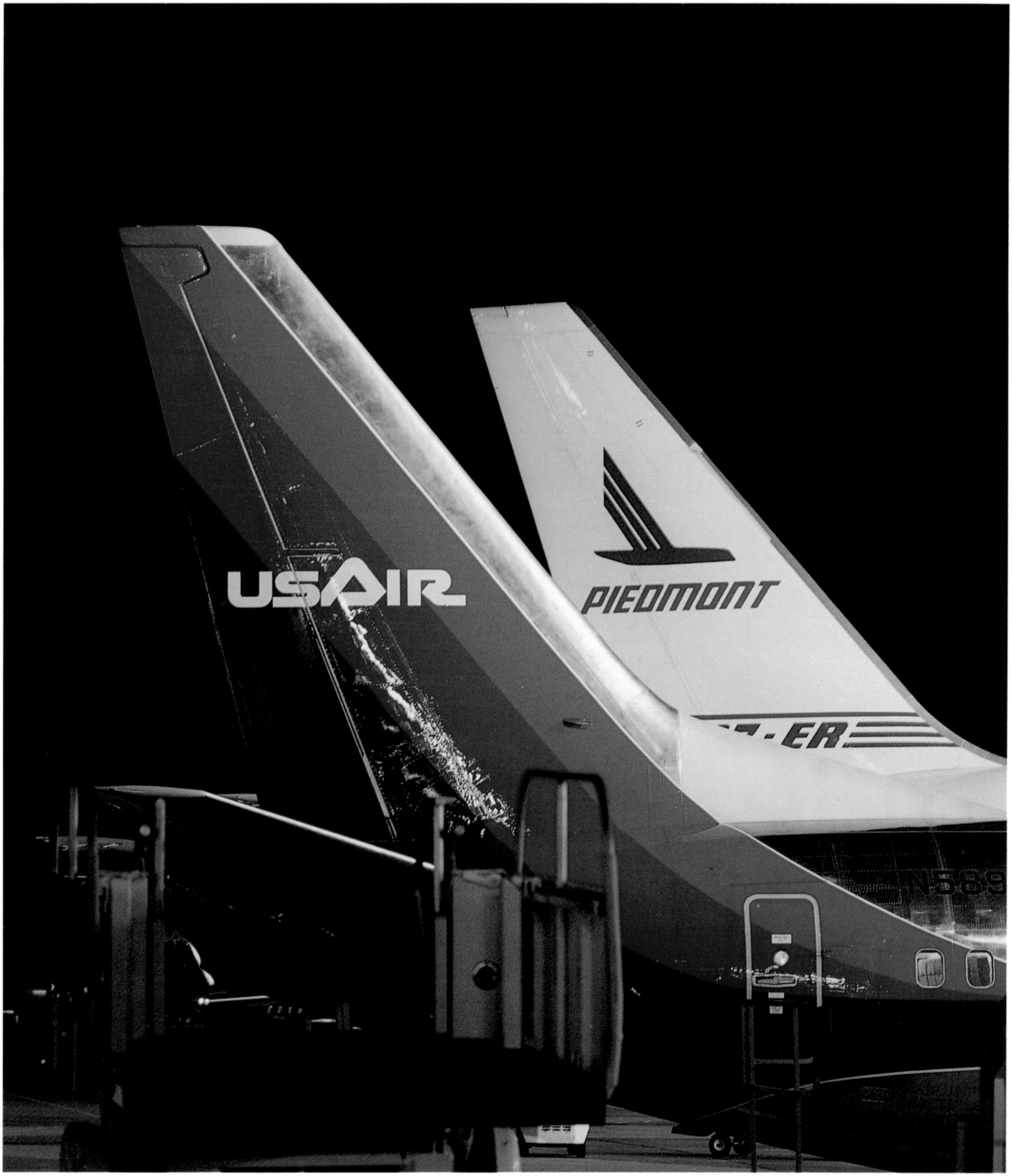
USAIR
PIEDMONT

Above A Piedmont Boeing 737-200 on approach to Miami International's Runway 9 Left in March 1989. Boeing's twin-jet short range transport first went into production in 1965. It is the most ordered jet airliner in history and there seems no reason why production of further stretched and developed versions of this workhorse of the US airline industry should not continue beyond the year 2000

Left Tails of the not so unexpected at Los Angeles Terminal 2 in January 1989 – a USAir 737-300 and a 767-200ER of Piedmont. North Carolina-based Piedmont was taken over by USAir in 1987, creating an airline with over 420 jet aircraft. Piedmont's operations, including its scheduled services to London, were completely integrated in 1989. USAir Group, the airline's parent company, also owns five major regional US commuter airlines, Henson, Jetstream, Pennsylvania Airlines, Suburban and Allegheny Commuter. From 1989 these feeder subsidiaries, plus CC Air, Chataqua, Crown, Commutair, Statewest and Air Midwest, have been marketed as USAir Express

Delta Airlines Boeing 737-300 on final approach to Runway 25 at Las Vegas. The aircraft was delivered new to Western Airlines in 1986, hence the registration suffix N312WA, which merged with all-conquering Delta in April 1987. When Atlanta-based Delta absorbed Western it became the third largest carrier in the USA. Then with it's purchase of Pan Am's Atlantic routes in September 1991, the airline was catapulted into becoming the world's largest passenger carrier (excluding Aeroflot), and the third largest revenue-earner. Founded in 1924 as a Mississippi crop-duster outfit (in fact the first agplane business in the world), Delta boomed in the 1950s in a period of rapid expansion through predatory takeovers of smaller rivals. In 1972 Delta took over Boston-based Northwest Airlines, inheriting a large fleet of 727s, DC-9s and FH-227 twinprops. But the really big leap for Delta came in 1987 when it took over Western Airlines, a company which traced its origin to the Western Air Transport Company founded in 1925 as an airmail carrier. Western had a merger flirtation with Continental in the 1970s, but a bid for growth after the de-regulation of the US airline industry left it short of funds and ripe for takeover by Delta. Delta operates from six major US hubs, with services provided throughout the USA to 160 destinations. Before the Pan Am takeover Delta was already flying international scheduled passenger services to Acapulco, Calgary, Dublin, Edmonton, Frankfurt, Guadlajara, Hamilton, Hamburg, Ixtapa, Juarez, London, Mazatlan, Mexico City, Montreal, Munich, Nassau, Paris, Puerto Vallarta, Seoul, Shannon, Stuttgart, Taipei, Tokyo and Vancouver. The takeover has opened up many more transatlantic route authorities and new destinations in the Middle East and India. An extensive feeder network is operated under the Delta Connection banner involving Cincinnati-based Comair, Boston, New York-based Business Express, Atlanta-based Atlantic Southwest and Salt Lake City Los Angeles-based Skywest. The Pan Am East Coast shuttle operations were recommenced under the Delta shuttle banner in September 1991

Boeing 737-300 N335AU in a one-off experimental paint scheme for USAir landing at Runway 9 Left at Fort Lauderdale, Florida, in March 1988. In November that year the aircraft was re-registered as N376US. USAir was established in 1939 as All American Aviation, changing its name to Allegheny in 1953, then to its present form in 1979. Its aquisition of Piedmont in 1987 turned the airline into a major force in the US regional sector. The airline suffered severe financial losses in 1991 but managed to pick up the leases of 10-ex-Eastern Boeing 757-200s and has ordered another 30 new-build aircraft from the manufacturers for mid-1990s delivery

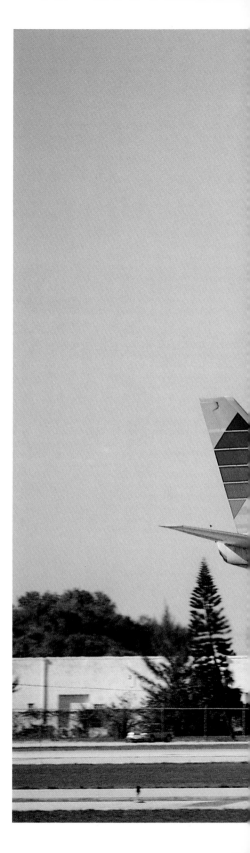

Above N453AC, a well-used Boeing 737-200 of American Airlines, on approach to Runway 25 Left at Los Angeles in January 1989. This aircraft was already over twenty years old when this shot was taken. It was first delivered to New Zealand National Airways in October 1968, passing later to various leasing operators. It operated with AirCal until the California-based carrier merged with American Airlines in July 1987. The take-over gave American an extensive route network along the US West Coast. Today, American's US-wide domestic network operates from five main hubs at Chicago, Dallas, Nashville, Raleigh/Durham and San Juan, and a sixth hub at San Jose opened in 1991. American flies international scheduled passenger services to London, Brussels, Dusseldorf, Frankfurt, Geneva, Hamburg, Lyon, Madrid, Manchester, Munich, Paris, Stockholm and Zürich, whilst operations across the Pacific from Dallas to Tokyo commenced in 1987. Other points are served in the Caribbean, Canada and Mexico. Their modern fleet includes Airbus A300-600Rs, Boeing 757-200s, 767-300ERs and a large number of MD-80s. More of these aircraft are on order, plus Fokkers 100s and MD-11s

Right Another American inheritance from the AirCal merger was this Boeing 737-300, delivered new in 1985. Here it is in American colours in February 1989, taxiing for take-off at John Wayne Airport, Orange County. America's parent organization, AMR, also controls a number of regional and commuter airlines which feed passengers into the bustling AA hubs under the marketing banner 'American Eagle'. These feeders include Air Midwest, AVAir, Command Airways, Simmons Airlines and Wings West. Other independents in the network are Chaparral Airlines, Executive Air Charter and Metroflight

Right Midway Airlines Boeing 737-200 N702ML on approach to Runway 9 Left at Fort Lauderdale, Florida, in March 1989. This aircraft, first flown in December 1979, had passed through many hands before arriving at Midway. This major US domestic regional operator began revenue earning services in 1979, absorbing Air Florida in 1984. The airline expanded rapidly with hubs at Chicago and Philadelphia, the latter opening in 1989 but was soon closed again after the airline hit commercial trouble – hit, so its management claimed, by massive price cutting by its floundering rival, Eastern. At its peak Midway was flying scheduled passenger services to 54 destinations in the eastern and southeast USA. There are two commuter subsidiaries, Iowa Airways and Midway Commuter, who jointly marketed under the banner the Midway Connection. In October 1991 Midway was taken over by Northwest, who planned to take over the leases on the airline's MD-80s and DC-9-30s. The Chicago-based airline's identity meanwhile would vanish

Above America West Boeing 737-300 at John Wayne, Orange County, in February 1989. Headquartered at Sky Harbor in the heart of the US 'sunbelt' America West operated from two major hubs – Phoenix and Las Vegas – flying scheduled services to destinations all over the mid and south-west, Texas and California. Passenger services are also flown to Minneapolis, Newark, Ontario, Washington DC and Honolulu

Left A much-travelled Boeing
737-200 of America West climbs
away from Las Vegas' hot and sticky
Runway 25 in February 1989.
Already 12 years old when caught on
camera, this aircraft had been
operated by Aloha, Nigeria Airways,
Western Airlines and Delta. First
leased to America West in June 1987
as N70721, the aircraft was re-
registered N195AW and bought by
the Polaris financing company and
subsequently leased back to the
Nevada-based carrier

Above American Airlines Boeing 737-300 begins its take-off roll along
Runway 25 Right at Los Angeles. Texas-based American Airlines is one of the
few success stories to have emerged from the US airline industry shake-out of
the late 1980s. From humble beginnings in 1934, it has grown into one of the
world's most significant air transport operations. America got its first postwar-
built equipment, Douglas DC-6s, into service in 1947 and began a major
modernization programme that would rapidly eclipse its competitors. Its war-
surplus DC-4s and DC-3s were retired by 1949 and replaced by Convair
CV-240 twinprops. The turboprop Lockheed Electra went into service in
January 1959, followed a few days later by the first Boeing 707, flying non-stop
from New York to Los Angeles. The new transcontinental jet service gave
American a tremendous edge over its rival United, which was still awaiting
delivery of its first DC-8s. American put turbofan powered Boeing 720Bs into
service in 1961, followed a year later by the exotic but ultimately unsuccessful
Convair CV-990 Coronado. American ordered the Boeing 747 off the
drawing board in 1967 and was an important launch customer for the Douglas
DC-10 in 1969

Above N664DN, a spanking new Delta Boeing 757-200 taxies to the airline's own gate at La Guardia, New York, in April 1991, just a few weeks after the airliner had left the production line. The twin-jet, two pilot, narrow- body 757 was originally planned as a redesigned 727, with advanced aerodynamics and two fuel efficient engines for maximum economy in a new era of high fuel prices. What emerged was a completely new aircraft. Following first prototype flight in 1982, Eastern was the 757's launch customer, commencing commercial service on 1 January 1983

Right Smoke puffs shroud the wheels at the moment of touch down for Eastern Boeing 757-225 N504EA at St Thomas, US Virgin Islands, after a direct flight from Miami in March 1988. Note the maker's big '757' in the Boeing 'Stratotype' typeface emblazoned on the tail to tell passengers they were flying in a comparatively new model, even though Eastern had operated this type for five years. This aircraft N504EA was delivered to Eastern in February 1983

Above An Eastern Boeing 757-225 takes on fuel into its capacious wing tanks at Miami International in April 1990

Left April 1990 and the prominent '757' has gone from the tail of Eastern's Boeing 757-225 N508EA as it taxies to the holding point of Runway 9 Left at Miami International. Miami-based Eastern was a prime casualty of the US airline shakeout, experiencing strikes and corporate raidings in the late 1980s. Texas Air took over the airline in 1986, and within two years had sold the New York-Washington shuttle, operated profitably by Eastern for 27 years to Trump. Eastern shrank dramatically in 1989-90 following an aircrew and engineer strike which grounded the airline for six months, after which it went into Chapter 11 bankruptcy. This gave the airline some commercial protection while sale of the aircraft and routes proceeded in a bid to survive. A large number of aircraft, plus Eastern's South American and Caribbean routes, were sold to American Airlines. Eastern ceased operations on January 18 1991. Easten had begun operations in 1926 as Pitcairn Aviation, being renamed Eastern Air Tranport three years later. It expanded rapidly by taking over smaller airlines – in 1967 it swallowed Miami-based Mackey and in 1974 it absorbed Caribair. In the 1960s Eastern flew more passengers than any other US airline, more than a million a month, and at its peak flew to 102 destinations. Over the years Eastern has been launch customer for important new aircraft such as the Lockheed Electra, Douglas DC-8-20 and the Boeing 757

Above The same aircraft, Boeing 767-231 N601TW approaches Runway 26 Left at Gatwick in this November 1985 photo. The medium range Boeing 767 has a wide -body, twin aisle fuselage and is offered in two models; the -200 series and the stretched -300 series, with passenger capacity increased by 45 to 250 + seats. The launch customer for the -200 was United Airlines, which flew its first commercial service with the type between Chicago and Denver in September 1982. Alternative engines from Pratt & Whitney and General Electric can be specified according to customer requirement, and the Rolls Royce RB211-524G became an option in 1990. Both 757 and 767 models are offered in standard and extended-range (ER) options with increased fuel capacity

Left Boeing 767-231 N601TW of TWA approaches Runway 25 Left at Los Angeles in February 1989. Delivered in November 1982, this was the airline's first 767 in service

Above Factory-fresh Boeing 767-300 N126DL of Delta Airlines glides over the fence for landing on General Electric CF6 power at Fort Lauderdale, Florida, in March 1988

Left A rare smog-free day in Los Angeles as a Boeing 767 'Luxuryliner' of American Airlines comes in to land on Runway 25 Left. This 767-223 Extended Range model, registered N322AA, was delivered to American in May 1986

DCs
and MDs

A veteran DC-8 of United Airlines passing over the 'piano keys', marking the beginning of the usable runway at Miami International, March 1988. This aircraft, registered N8079U, was first delivered to United in March 1968 as a -61 model. The aircraft was re-engined with GE-SNECMA CFM56 turbofans as a DC-8-71 in July 1983. Cammacorp Inc undertook a large scale programme in the early 1980s re-engining 'Super Sixty' series Douglas jets enabling them to operate for years more. Many were converted into freighters

Above United DC-8-71 on final approach to Runway 30, Miami International

Left DC-8-71 of United Airlines on approach to Las Vegas Runway 25 in February 1989

Above N2874 United Airlines passenger carrying DC-8-71

Left A DC-8-71 series of Delta Airlines caught by the camera in March 1988 about to recover on Miami's Runway 30

Above DC-8-51 of Connie Kalitta airlines on the cargo ramp just south of the threshold of Runway 25 Left, Los Angeles Airport, in January 1989 preparing for its nocturnal duties flying parcel freight across the US. This aircraft has a long history, having been first delivered to Delta in June 1962, registered N809E. It was then operated by Maldives International (later Air Maldives) and stored at Malé since 1985. Its present owner bought the aircraft in 1987 and the registration was changed to N805CK. Connie Kalitta Services Inc, an all-cargo airline based at Willow Run airport, Ypsilanti, Michigan, was founded in 1965 by Mr Conrad Kalitta and operates 12 DC-8 freighters, plus Learjets and Turbo Beech 18s

Left Eastern DC-9-31 N8920E seconds away from touch down onto Miami's Runway 30 Right, a moment captured in March 1988. This aircraft was first delivered in March 1967. It was withdrawn from service and put into storage at Marana, Arizona the desert maintenance and aircraft holding centre run by Evergreen International in September 1988

Above McDonnell Douglas MD-82 of TWA on final approach to Runway 22 Right, JFK, New York, in April 1991. The MD-80 family stems directly from the DC-9, which made its maiden flight in Febraury 1965. The DC-9-80, renamed with the new McDonnell-Douglas styled prefix, first flew in 1980. All members of the MD-80 family, with varying fuselage lengths and passenger capacity use the same wing and the Pratt & Whitney JT8D-200 series of engines

Left TWA MD-82 on the parallel taxyway near the holding point of Runway 9 Left, Fort Lauderdale, Florida

Above American Airlines MD-82 on approach to Phoenix Runway 8 Right, in February 1989. This aircraft was first delivered to the airline in September 1984

Left Passengers board an American Airlines MD-80 at John Wayne Airport, Orange County, California, on a flight bound for Dallas/Fort Worth

The Hilton Hotel north of the Runways 8 and 26 Left and Right at Hartsfield Airport, Atlanta, Georgia, provides the backdrop as an MD-80 of American Airlines taxies towards the AA gate

This McDonnell Douglas MD-81, registered N849HA and seen here in Continental markings departing Las Vegas in Febraury 1989, already had a long list of owners. Originally delivered to Hawaiian in 1983 and named 'Kailua Kona', the aircraft had been leased to American International Airways, repossessed by Hawaiian, then operated by Frontier Airlines until the carrier was swallowed by Continental in 1987

Above MD-83 N939AS of Alaska Airlines flares over the threshold of Runway 26 Left at Sky Harbor airport, Phoenix, Arizona. This shot was taken in February 1989

Right Flying the flag, an Alaska Airlines MD-83 climbs away from Burbank Glendale Pasadena Airport north-bound for Seattle in February 1989. The airport, which is utilised by the Lockheed factory, is a domestic-only facility serving northern Los Angeles' busy commuter and regional traffic

The heavies

Action at Miami International, as Pan Am's *Clipper Tradewind* a 1970-vintage Boeing 747-100, registered N4712U is pushed back from the international satellite on a March evening in 1988. The streams of light behind are aircraft finishing their landing roll on Runway 9 Right. Pan Am, like other major US airlines, flew into the financial turbulence at the outset of the 1990s, hampered by crippling losses made through the preceding decade and an ageing fleet. Pan American World Airways was founded in 1927 and rapidly grew into one of the world's greatest airlines, pushing its route network into Latin America and across the Atlantic. After World War 2, Pan Am was first with the new generation of US piston-powered transport aircraft—the Constellation, the DC-6, the Boeing Stratocruiser and the DC-7C. Pan Am ordered the Boeing 707 in 1955 just a year after the first flight of the revolutionary Boeing Jet Transport and flew the first revenue-earning flight, from New York to Paris, on 26 October 1956, heralding the jet age of mass civil air transport. Pan Am was first too into the wide-body age, placing an order off the drawing board in 1966 for 25 Boeing 747s. The first 747-121 started commercial service with a non-stop flight from New York to London on January 21, 1970. Some of these ageing first batch aircraft were still in service with the airline when it was overcome by financial crisis, unable to replace them.

De-regulation at the end of the 1970s allowed Pan Am to build a domestic network after years of being shut out of the internal US market. There was a short cut to this end when Pan Am took control of Miami-based National Airlines, who operated a large route network around the eastern seaboard and Gulf coast, plus ready-made trans-US services. In 1986, under severe cash constraints, the airline sold its entire Pacific division to United Airlines. In the summer of 1991 every division of the cash-starved airline was put up for sale with bids from United, Delta, TWA and American Airlines. Delta won the prize of Pan Am's transatlantic routes and its Frankfurt hub, leaving the depleted airline, itself now 45 per cent owned by Delta, with just its Latin American operations, where ironically the airline had first taken off as a world force sixty years before

Clipper Tradewind awaits push-back clearance on the stand at Miami. This aircraft had been first delivered to United in 1970 and named *The Original Eight,* then bought by Pan Am in 1985. A side cargo door was fitted in September 1988

Clipper Ocean Herald, a Boeing 747-100 of Pan Am, approaches JFK in April 1991, bearing troops returning from *Operation Desert Storm* in the deserts of Arabia, (as indicated by the 'yellow ribbon' motif painted just above and to the left of the front starboard door). Large numbers of long range airliners were mobilized by the US Civil Reserve Air Fleet to fly service personnel to and from the Gulf war zone from the continental United States and Europe. This aircraft dates from 1970. In 1971 it had been briefly leased to Eastern Airlines

Above Pan Am Boeing 747 climbs away from Heathrow's Runway 27 Left on a morning in August 1989, its main undercarriage doors just closing

Left Pan Am *Clipper Ocean Spray* leads another 747 of the same airline to the holding point of Runway 9 Right at Heathrow sometime in June 1989. One of the very earliest 747-100 models built, this aircraft was delivered in 1970 and named *Clipper Star of the Union*. The aircraft was given its new name in 1980

Left Boeing 747 of Continental Airlines awaiting departure clearance from Gatwick's Runway 8 Left, transatlantic bound for Newark, New Jersey, on a fine day in June 1989. Since the first commercial flight from New York to London on 21 January 1970, fourteen different versions of the 747 have entered service. The latest, the 747-400 Combi became available early in 1989 and a fifteenth variant, the 747-400 Freighter, is due for delivery to Air France in 1993

Above N603PE, a well-used Boeing 747-100 of Continental, rotates off Runway 27 Right at Miami International on a spring evening in 1988. This aircraft had first been delivered 18 years earlier to Alitalia, passing through Hawaii Express and the Flying Tiger Line , before becoming N603PE with People Express in the summer of 1984. In February 1987 the no-frills cut-price carrier merged with Continental

Above Tower Air Boeing 747-121 N604FF approaches to land at JFK. The airline brought this very early 100 series jet out of storage at Marana, Arizona in 1988 where it was laid up after 18 years' service with Pan Am. It had first flown in 1970 as *Clipper Sovereign of the Seas.* New York based Tower Air, founded in 1983, operates a fleet of four -100 series Boeing 747s on scheduled flights from JFK to Israel, and from New York and Miami to Scandinavia

Left Before the merger with Continental, this People Express Boeing 747-143 was caught by the camera approaching Gatwick in November 1985. This aircraft already had a long history, having flown with Alitalia as I-DEME, thereafter with Aer Lingus, SAS, Scanair, Icelandair, Air Algérie, Overseas National Airways and PIA – all with the US registrastion N356AS. In June 1985 it became N606PE with People Express, which merged with Continental in February 1987

Boeing 747-131 of TWA, registered N93107, climbing away from Heathrow. This aircraft had first been delivered to the airline in 1970. Trans World Airlines, one of the most famous names in airline history, was struggling for commercial survival at the end of 1990 as losses mounted in the teeth of a worldwide industry recession deepened by the Gulf War. In January 1991 American Airlines agreed to buy TWA's routes from the US to London, Gatwick in a cash-raising bid and that summer, the airline failed on its attempt to merge with the struggling Pan Am. The once-mighty airline was formed on 1 October 1930 as Transcontinental and Western Air, with a key contract to fly air mail on a multi-stop trans-America route from New York to Los Angeles, which effectively subsidised the passenger operation. The airline commissioned a new transport aircraft from Douglas which emerged as the single prototype Douglas DC-1 in July 1933. The first of 20 follow-on DC-2s was delivered in mid-1934, the new aircraft being capable of performing transcontinental mail flights in 18 hours. The larger DC-3 joined the TWA fleet in 1936, followed by the first of five Boeing Model 307 Stratoliners in 1940. In 1939 Howard Hughes bought a large block of the company's stock. The mercurial millionaire pushed for a long range luxurious aircraft that would emerge as the Constellation, and spurred some heated boardroom rows. The post-war air travel boom saw TWA opening intercontinental routes via Gander and Shannon to London and Paris and to North Africa and China, the carrier officially re-titling itself Trans World Airways in 1950. After a series of boardroom battles with the increasingly eccentric Howard Hughes he was forced to surrender his control. TWA had managed meanwhile to get into the jet age early with the entry into service of its first Boeing 707-131, flying non-stop from San Francisco to New York on 20 March 1959. In 1965 Boeing 727s began operations on domestic services, followed by DC-9s. In 1971 TWA entered the wide-body era with its first Boeing 747-100s and Lockheed L-1011 TriStars

Right Boeing 747 of TWA, registered N53116, landing at Heathrow in January 1991, almost 20 years after it was first delivered to the airline. TWA's commercial problems of the 1980s were accelerated by its ageing fleet. In September 1985 the airline was taken over by the Wall Street entrepreneur Carl Icahn, who acquired 52 per cent of the company's shares. TWA has been in and out of profit since the takeover but has not been able to substantially modernise its ageing fleet. The company took over the St Louis based Ozark Air Lines in 1987. The airline's route network connects over 100 destinations within the USA with the airline's main hubs at St Louis and New York, JFK. Transatlantic services are operated to the major cities of western Europe

Above With its gear down, a United Airlines Boeing 747SP approaches Runway 25 Left at Los Angeles in this February 1989 photo. The short-fuselage SP was developed by Boeing for reduced passenger seat-mile costs on very long range flights. Pan Am was the first SP customer and inaugurated non-stop New York-Tokyo flights in 1976. Ten years later Pan Am sold its transpacific routes along with 10 747-21s to United, plus a single ex-Braniff 747SP-27. United Airlines, founded in March 1931 from four pioneer operators, had always been a dynamic force in the US airline industry. It had put advanced Boeing Model 247 all-metal monoplanes into service in 1932 and introduced stewardesses, plus galley cooked in-flight meals and sleeper accommodation before World War 2. As the jet age dawned, the airline briefly considered buying DH Comets but ordered DC-8s instead. The Douglas jet tranports entered service in 1961, the year United took over Capital Airlines with a fleet of turboprop Viscounts. United ordered French-built Caravelles as its first medium range jets, later supplanted by 727s. The first wide-body 747s were ordered in 1966. Today the airline operates from five major hubs at Washington, Chicago, Denver, San Francisco and Narita (Tokyo). United flies a large network of scheduled passenger services linking 154 destinations in the USA, Canada and Mexico with international services to the Far East, Australia and New Zealand

Left Boeing 747-45, registered N661US, in the striking new livery of Northwest Airlines introduced in 1989, on approach to Runway 31 Right at JFK in April 1991, two years after going into service. Northwest was the launch customer for the advanced -400 series with its easily recognizable 6-foot high winglets, plus the not so readily visible, but highly significant advances to airframe and flight controls beneath the skin. This, the first -400 series aircraft to be delivered, had originally flown as N401PW, the registration chosen to publicise the Pratt & Whitney PW4000 series engines. On 27 June 1988 this aircraft set an official weight record by reaching an altitude of 2000 metres at a gross weight of 892,450 lbs

Above Northwest put its first 747-400 series onto domestic flights in early 1989 before starting long-haul international operations with the new aircraft later that year on its transpacific routes. Here in February 1989 a 747-451 registered N663US climbs away from Phoenix's Sky Harbor airport bound for Minneapolis-St Paul. The new 747-400 offers a 7-11 per cent reduction in fuel-burn per seat compared with that of the 747-300, and up to 25 per cent reduction compared with older 747 models. Northwest has placed large orders for Airbus aircraft including the A340, the European-built rival to the latest model Boeing 747.

Left Inside the purpose-built 747 final assembly hangar at Boeing's Everett plant, situated north of Seattle in Washington state in the northeast USA. Left to right are a -200 series for ANA Japan, a -400 for Northwest and another -400 for British Airways

Above N470EV, a Boeing 747-273C freighter of Evergreen International Airlines, waits nose-up at a JFK cargo ramp in April 1991. This factory-built, fully convertible passenger-cargo variant was first delivered to World Airways in June 1974, then variously leased to Korean, Braniff, VIASA, Lufthansa, American Airlines and Flying Tigers until bought by Evergreen in May 1987. The all-cargo airline, known as Johnson Flying Services until 1975, was founded in 1924. Today it operates worldwide freight charters with a fleet of five 747s, 12 727s, three DC-8s and eight DC-9s. Evergreen also flies for United Parcel Services and the US Mail, and operates a Hong Kong-New York cargo service

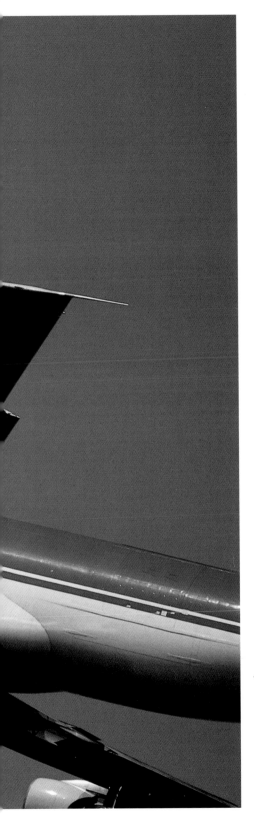

Left Even flying parcel freight can be glamorous, and in the US airline shoot-outs of the 1980s it has proved a much more reliable way to make a buck than flying people. In this shot Federal Express Boeing 747-249F package-freighter registered N631FE and dubbed *Robert W Prescott* departs JFK in April 1991, climbing out over Rockaway beach on Long Island. This aircraft had originally been delivered to Flying Tiger Line as N806FT. FedEx specializes in door-to-door collection and delivery of parcels and packages with a standard ceiling of 68 kg in weight, or 3.3 metres in combined length and girth, and offers a range of ranked-priority services. The operational centre is at Memphis International Airport, Tennessee, from where loads are despatched every night all over the USA. There are other hubs at Newark and Oakland. Operations began in 1973 with a small fleet of Falcon 20 biz-jets. De-regulation of the US air cargo industry in 1977 allowed long-range services to be opened up, while a very large fleet of over 200 single-engined Cessnas was progressively acquired to fly the delivery and collection 'spokes' from the trunk hubs. The fleet includes 20 Boeing 747-100F and 200Fs, 160 Boeing 727s, 24 McDonnell Douglas DC-10s, and six DC-8-73Fs. Federal Express had ordered 25 Airbus A300-600F freighters to replace its earlier model 727s on internal US domestic routes on a one-for-two basis, with a promised 40 per cent gain in capacity

Above Boeing 747-2R7F of Flying Tigers landing at Miami International in March 1988. This aircraft was purpose-built by Boeing as a frieghter without windows, with a nose 'visor' as Boeing call the nose-door, and with a side cargo door behind the wing. It was first delivered to the Luxembourg-based freight carrier Cargolux in January 1979

Above N92GS, a Boeing 720-047B of Miami-based carrier Pan Aviation, has its engines serviced. This aircraft, fitted out as an executive transport, was withdrawn from use in 1990 and put into store at this general purpose freight and charter operator's compound in Miami. The Boeing 720 was a short-range re-design of the 707. This aircraft had originally been delivered to Western Airlines in 1962. In the backgound is a Surinam Airways Douglas DC-8

Left Flying Tiger tails in the Los Angeles maintenance area in February 1989. When this photo was taken, the Tigers' days were numbered as a bravely independent operator. That year Federal Express bought out the famous all-freight airline established in 1945 as National Skyways Freight Corporation by a group of ex-US Army Air Force pilots. The buy-out of the California-based Flying Tiger Line with its fleet of Boeing 747 freighters and extensive air cargo operations in the Pacific Rim, Asia and Latin America, catapulted FedEx to the position of the largest air freight carrier in the world. By sales it ranks number eleven in the world and in 1990 was the world's thirteenth fastest growing airline

A DC-8 plunges majestically out of
the Florida sunset on approach to
Miami International

Above Continental DC-10-10 registered N68046, and friends at Los Angeles Terminal 6 early in 1989. This -10 series Douglas tri-jet had first been delivered to Continental in 1973. The DC-10 tri-jet programme was launched in 1968 with large orders from United for the initial DC-10-10 model, which first flew in August 1970.

Left Continental DC-10-30, registered N14063, departs Gatwick Runway 26 Left bound for Houston. This shot was taken in 1985; the black tail logo has since changed to red. This aircraft had already passed through several operators' hands. First delivered to Alitalia as I-DYNO in November 1973, it had been leased to Sabena, bought back by the manufacturers, then sold on to Continental in 1984. The intercontinental range Model -30 first flew in June 1972 and a total of 174 DC-10-30s and -30ERs, and 35 DC-10-30 freighters were built before production finally ended in 1988

Above United DC-10-30 flares over Runway 12 at Miami International in March 1989. The dominance of Pan Am at the time at MIA is made evident by the cluster of tails in the background. In spite of its commercial troubles, Pan Am shrewdly concentrated investment on its Miami hub as a bridgehead into the Caribbean and Latin America

Left Welcome to LA on an early spring morning in 1989 as N1805U, a DC-10-10 of United Airlines, waits for take-off clearance, lined up on Los Angeles' Runway 25 Right. A USAir MD-82 meanwhile makes its final descent onto Runway 24 Right

Above American Airlines DC-10-10 awaits take-off clearance on Runway 25 Right at Los Angeles. The lights in the foregound mark Runway 25 Left which is nearer to the perimeter of the airfield. This runway is generally used for less noisy arrivals, which is standard noise abatement procedure at many US airports with twin parallel runways

Left Hot but getting higher, this American Airlines DC-10-10 rotates off Runway 25 Left at Las Vegas, shimmering in the mid-afternoon heat of the Nevada desert

Above A TWA Lockheed L-1011 TriStar 50, registered N31023, on final approach to Runway 22 Right at JFK. This aircraft originally flew in June 1974 and was converted from TriStar 1 to -50 standard in April 1981. The TriStar was never quite a soaraway success as an airliner. Its prospects looked rosier at the end of the 1960s when Lockheed studied new transports for the wide-body age, the company choosing a tri-jet layout after intensive market research showed the excellent prospects for a short to medium range mass people mover. American Airlines were the driver of the project with a 1966 requirement for a 300-seater to operate the Chicago-Los Angeles route at maximum efficiency. Lockheed chose the as yet unproven Rolls-Royce RB.211 turbofan as the powerplant because of its promised fuel economy. Early difficulties with the RB.211 led to the financial collapse of the British engine maker in 1971 and huge problems for Lockheed, beaten by their rivals in getting wide-bodies to their airline customers. Frustrated by the delay, American Airlines eventually bought the DC-10-10 instead, which went into first revenue earning service on the Chicago-LA route on 5 August 1971

Left A DC-10-30 Federal Express package-freighter captured in a busy night-time scene in early 1989 on the FedEx ramp at Los Angeles – positioned just to the south of Runway 25 Left, on the intersection of Imperial Highway and Sepulveda Boulevard

Above TWA L-1011 TriStar 50 N81027 departs Heathrow on a sunny
afternoon in October 1985. This aircraft had also been converted from TriStar 1
to 50 standard in mid-1981. The prototype TriStar flew on 16 November 1971.
The first revenue earning flights were made by Eastern in April 1972 and by
TWA a few days later, both flying the first production model, the L-1011-1.
The L-1011-100, which entered service in 1975, is an extended range model
with extra fuel carried in centre section tanks. The L- 1011-200 model which
followed was powered by RB.211-524 engines, which delivered improved take-
off and climb performances from hot-and-high airfields and longer range. The
-500 model introduced a substantial improvement in range. In contrast to the
normal stretch process of developing aircraft, the 500's airframe was shortened
with a five-metre chop in a fuselage now accommodating 246 standard and 300
high density passengers. Maximum range with a full load was, however,
pushed out to over 9600 km on the power of three RB.211-524Bs. The first
L-1011-500 entered service in May 1979 with British Airways. The last
TriStar was delivered in 1983

Right Hawaiian Air's flamboyant tail logo caught on a L-1011 Tri Star 1 at
Los Angeles in early 1989. Based at Honolulu, Hawaiian flies to the USA,
Europe and the Far East. Along with TriStars, Hawaiian operates DC-8s, DC-9s
and DHC Dash-7s on inter-island flights

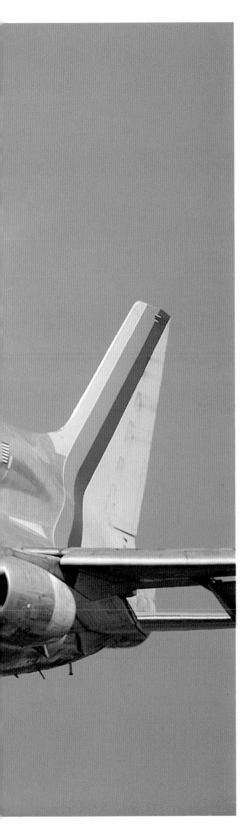

Above N724DA, a TriStar 200 of Delta Airlines, rises from Runway 26 Left at Gatwick on a clear day in late 1985

Left An Eastern Airlines TriStar on approach to Runway 30 at Miami International in March 1988

European invasion

Left Airbus A300B4 registered N202EA of Eastern Airlines on finals to Miami's Runway 30. Airbus Industrie was set up at the outset of the 1970s as a collaborative Western European effort to be a counterweight to the growing US dominance of world airliner production. The first Airbus product was the A300, a large capacity short-to-medium range transport of which over three hundred and thirty are in world airline service

Below Burning rubber, an Eastern Airbus A300 touches down on Miami's Runway 30, puffs of smoke billowing momentarily from the big airliner's tyres, as another Eastern Airbus climbs into the sky from Runway 27 Right

An Airbus A300 N232EA of Eastern
Airlines unloads cargo pallets at
night at Miami's International
satellite stand E31. This aircraft,
finished in Eastern's original white
colour scheme rather than bare metal,
was delivered to the airline at the end
of 1983. In the background a British
Airways Boeing 747 taxies from left
to right towards the Runway 9 Right
holding point, before taking off for
Heathrow. In the distant sky a lone
aircraft makes its approach to
Runway 9 Left

Above American Airlines A300B4-605R, registered N80052, taxies towards Runway 12 holding point, Miami International in April 1990. The A300-600 is the largest twin-engined aircraft to win the three hour EROPS (extended range twin engine) clearance, which allows the aircraft to be operated over long-range sectors previously confined to three- or four-engined types

Left Looming out of the evening sky, an Eastern Airlines A300B4-203, registered N224EA, approaches Miami

An Airbus A300B4-203 of Pan Am, *Clipper Detroit* taxies to line up at bustling Runway 9 Left, Miami. Originally ordered for Air Jamaica, the Toulouse-built airliner was leased to Pan Am in May 1985

Above Night scene at Houston International airport where Continental Airbus A300B4-103, N210EA (originally delivered to Eastern in 1979) is pushed back from the stand. A three-minute exposure captured this scene in January 1989

Left An Airbus A310-324 of Pan Am *Clipper Plymouth Rock* awaits instructions to line up at Heathrow on a bright morning in January 1991. First flown in 1988 as F-WWCD, the aircraft was re-registered N820PA in US airline service

Pan Am Airbus A310 N820PA on approach to Heathrow. Pan Am used its Airbus fleet primarily on its once-thriving European internal routes – sold off when the airline hit its deepening cash crisis in 1989. The 250-seat 310 has a shorter fuselage than the A300, using the same fuselage cross section but has new advanced technology wings, common engine pylons able to support a range of different engine options and an advanced two-man cockpit. Pan Am ordered the 310-300 extended range version in 1986. In March 1990 so-called EROPS (extended range operations) certification was obtained from the relevant US and European licensing authorities for the twin-engined A300 and A310 types using GE CF6-80C2 engines for flights which would take the flightpath up to 180 minutes from the nearest suitable airport in the case of an emergency. The A310 with Pratt & Whitney PW4152 engines was awarded 120 min EROPS clearance

Pan Am Airbus A310-324 *Clipper Midnight Sun* about to land at Heathrow, January 1991. Pan Am had taken delivery of this aircraft in October 1987

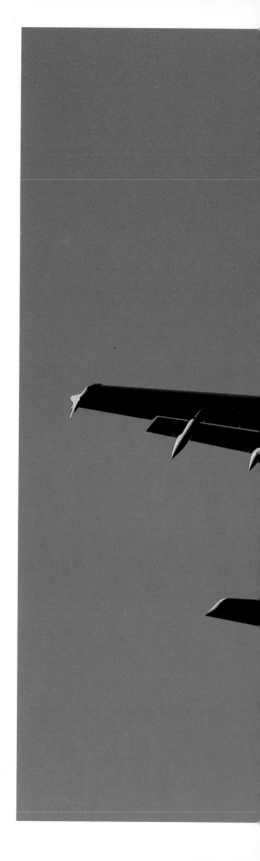

Above Bustling activity at John Wayne Airport, Orange County, California in early 1989. Two BAe 146s of American Airlines with a single-engine Cessna getting airborne. American acquired six BAe 146-200s with its takeover of Air Cal in July 1987

Right American Airlines ground crew hitch up the air tug for the push-back of a BAe 146 at Orange County, just south of Long Beach

Above USAir BAe 146-200 N178US about to land at Las Vegas. The aircraft had originally been delivered to Pacific Southwest Airlines, which merged with the regional giant in 1987

Left BAe 146-200 of USAir, registered N178US, approaches Las Vegas in Febraury 1989 – the tailcone airbrake has not yet deployed. USAir inherited its 19-strong fleet of BAe 146-200s when it took over Pacific Southwest Airlines. But the airline had to reduce the number of seats in the British-built short range airliner from 100 to 81 to meet customer comfort demand in the busy and highly competitive 'West Coast corridor'. In Spring 1991 the airline withdrew the type, claiming they were uneconomical and cancelled the lease contracts involving a $44 million write-off. After a year of enduring losses USAir dropped six California airports from its operations; Burbank, Oakland, Ontario, Orange County, Palm Springs and San José, and axed its hub operation at Cleveland. American Airlines also announced it was withdrawing from the Los-Angeles-San Francisco shuttle section of the corridor because of ferocious price-cutting by competitors

N146AC, a BAe 146-200 of
American Airlines, wears a hastily
adapted scheme following the merger
with Air Cal. The commuter airliner
was pictured at John Wayne in
January 1989. The Orange County,
California, airport imposes some of
the strictest noise regulations in the
world, giving the exceptionally quiet
British-built jet airliner its first toe-
hold in the US

Ten minutes in the life of Los Angeles airport – night traffic caught with
a time exposure